ROLE-PLAYING FOR FUN AND PROFIT™

ZOMBIE RUNS

JOE GREEK

rosen publishing's
rosen
central®

New York

Published in 2016 by The Rosen Publishing Group, Inc.
29 East 21st Street, New York, NY 10010

Copyright © 2016 by The Rosen Publishing Group, Inc.

First Edition

Library of Congress Cataloging-in-Publication Data

Greek, Joe.
 Zombie runs / Joe Greek.
    pages cm -- (Role-playing for fun and profit)
 Includes bibliographical references and index.
 ISBN 978-1-4994-3738-6 (library bound) -- ISBN 978-1-4994-3736-2 (pbk.) -- ISBN
 978-1-4994-3737-9 (6-pack)
 1. Running--Juvenile literature. 2. Zombies--Juvenile literature. 3. Role playing--Juvenile literature. I. Title.
 GV1061.G68 2016
 796.42
 [23]
                                     2015022785

Manufactured in the United States of America

INTRODUCTION

The growing popularity of zombies among all ages has led many peop[le] to blend other enjoyable activities with zombie lore, including physical fitness and charity runs!

Imagine for a moment that you're walking with friends through a local park. The sun is shining and the breeze feels cool on your face. Suddenly from behind, you hear a low rumbling noise. You turn around, and you recognize the sound. It's the sound of many people moaning.

Then, over a hill, the source of the noise appears. Staggering and limping slowly along, dozens of pallid-looking men, women, and young people are headed your way. Their clothes are ripped, and there is blood dripping from their mouths. The horde is nearly on you. As the bodies slowly shuffle forward, they make strange hisses and snarls and reach out to grab you. Eventually the entire crowd moves off while you and your friends look at each other in wonder. What you just saw wasn't a scene from a monster movie—you just experienced a zombie run!

Zombie runs are fun events that are happening all around the world. Emerging from the recent interest in zombie lore, competitive and non-competitive events are growing more people. Inspired by Hollywood hits, such as the film *Night of the Living Dead* (1968) and the television series *The Walking Dead*, as well as the growing interest in cosplay, it was only a matter of time before people started to dress up like zombies for public events.

The best part about zombie runs is that enthusiasts of all ages can get involved. Additionally, they don't have to involve running at all. Many zombie runs are slow walks that are held to raise awareness for a charity. Some events, however, may involve lots of physical activity and require being in good shape to compete.

Finding a zombie event, as you will learn, is quite easy. With the Internet, finding a horde of zombies that plan to march through town can require just a few simple searches.

In the following sections, we will also discuss how you can plan your own zombie run with friends and family. There are many tasks that have to be completed, including setting rules and promoting the event.

Finally, we will also talk about how you can turn your own interest in zombies and zombie events into a career. It may surprise you how many different career paths are related to zombie runs. From becoming an actor to planning large events, including conventions and weddings, zombie runs can open the door to a future job. So get ready to join the horde as you learn more about zombie runs.

CHAPTER ONE

WHEN THE DEAD WALK AGAIN

Zombies have fascinated moviegoers and readers for several decades. From fears of what nuclear war and strange viruses can do to the human body—alive or dead—the understanding of what a zombie is has greatly evolved throughout history. Today, zombies are a part of popular culture around the world. From thrilling television shows to horrifying survival games, zombies just keep on coming. In the following sections, we will discuss the origins of zombie lore and how movies, books, and videogames have created generations of fans that are becoming involved in real-world zombie games.

DEAD HISTORY

Today, we tend to associate the term zombie with Hollywood films about plagues and nuclear war. However, the word can actually be traced back to slaves who were brought from Africa to the Caribbean. Between 1625 and 1804, the African slave trade thrived on various Caribbean islands. One island, Haiti,

When African people were brought to the Caribbean and forced into slavery, they brought their religious practices. In Haiti, this became a religion called vodou where practitioners could cast spells on victims.

was under French colonial rule, and men, women, and children were forced to work on sugar plantations. Even though they had lost their freedom, many of these people brought their beliefs, including religious customs, to Haiti. The mixture of beliefs of the African slaves, the indigenous people, and the Europeans who enslaved them helped lead to the creation of a religion that became known as vodou.

According to Haitian folklore, a vodou sorcerer called a bokor can create a zombie by casting a spell. Unlike the walking dead that we think of today, vodou zombies are said to be living people who have been given a dose of non-fatal poison. Supposedly, victims of a bokor's spell will go into a trance and do anything that is asked of them.

Over time, however, the idea of zombies evolved as more cultures became fascinated with them. Rather than referring to living people put under the spell of a sorcerer, the term eventually became used to describe reanimated bodies of the dead.

THE ZOMBIE POP-CULTURE PHENOMENON

Through the 1800s and into the first half of the 20th century, the term still primarily referred to people put under spells. In America, the term was used in a racial and racist sense. According to National Public Radio, an essay by Ann Kordas notes that by the mid-1800s, a zombie for many had "come to be associated with a creature of African origin that willingly performed services for whites."

In 1936, zombies made their Hollywood debut in the film *White Zombie*. Directed by Victor and Edward Halperin, the film tells the story of a young woman put under the spell of a vodou sorcerer. Not very popular among audiences of the time, *White Zombie* is now considered a classic among zombie fans.

The 1968 film *Night of the Living Dead* is generally credited with popularizing the genre of zombie films and books that we enjoy today. Directed by George A. Romero, the movie changed the image of zombies, but it also broke down racial barriers of the time. Rarely seen in Hollywood until that point, the film's lead actor was played by African American Duane Jones.

GEORGE A. ROMERO

Born in New York in 1940, Romero is best known for his contributions as a director, writer, and producer in the horror movie genre. After graduating from college in 1961, Romero filmed segments for the popular children's series *Mr. Rogers' Neighborhood*. His low-budget zombie film *Night of the Living Dead* was not successful in theatres when it was released, but it is now recognized as a horror masterpiece. Romero's vision of zombies as slow-moving corpses inspired generations of directors and writers to follow in the same path.

Romero has frequently worked together with horror writer Stephen King. Together they have put out several horror films, including *Knightriders* (1981) and *Creepshow* (1982). Spanning more than four decades, Romero continues to write and direct zombie films, such as *Survival of the Dead* (2009).

Released during the civil rights movement that had gripped American society, Romero later said that he heard the news of Martin Luther King's assassination the night editing of the film was finished. Many zombie films would follow in Romero's steps to provide social commentary rather than pure fright.

Throughout the 80s and 90s, interest in the zombie genre slowed down. But in the 2000s, the genre made a comeback. Films such as the fast-paced horror thriller *28 Days Later* (2002) and comedy *Shaun of the Dead* (2004) put zombie films in a different light. The television series *The Walking Dead,* which premiered on October 31, 2010, took audiences by storm. For its season five premiere in 2014, 17.3 million viewers tuned in, making it the most watched show ever up to that point.

THE GROWING WORLD OF ZOMBIE FICTION

For nearly as long as humans have been writing, the idea that the dead could walk among the living has been written about. *The Epic of Gilgamesh*, a poem that dates back to 2000 BCE, makes possibly the earliest reference to what we think of as modern-day zombies.

"I will knock down the Gates of the Netherworld,
I will smash the door posts, and leave the doors flat down,
and will let the dead go up to eat the living!
And the dead will outnumber the living!"

After Haiti won its independence from France in 1804, becoming only the second independent country in the Americas, travel writers began making mention of zombies in newspaper articles and books. William Seabrook's *The Magic Island* (1929) earned mainstream success. In his book, Seabrook writes about encountering vodou cults on the island. He is often credited for popularizing the term zombie.

Until the 1980s, zombie literature failed to gain the popularity seen by movies. In 1989, however, editors John Skipp and Craig Spector published the popular anthology of horror stories *Book of the Dead.* Following in the footsteps of films that embraced end-of-the-world scenarios, readers became obsessed.

In 2003, writer Robert Kirkman and artist Tony Moore released the first comic book of the *The Walking Dead* series, which was turned into the television show. That same year, Max Brooks published *The Zombie Survival Guide.* A manual for surviving zombie attacks and the end of civilization, the book became a New York Times best seller. Brooks also published *World War Z: An Oral History of the Zombie War* (2006), which was turned into a 2013 film starring Brad Pitt.

ZOMBIES IN THE VIRTUAL WORLD

With the dead taking over movies and books, it's only fitting that they have a place in video games. One of the most popular zombie video game series is the *Resident Evil* franchise, which first hit shelves in 1996. Having sold millions of games, the series has revolved around different groups of survivors who battle zombies and other monsters created by a virus. The worldwide popularity of the series eventually led to the equally successful movie series of the same name.

In recent years, the Internet and technology have made it possible for large numbers of people to play zombie survival games together. *Day Z* (2013) is a massively multiplayer online (MMO) game where players work together or against each other in order to survive hordes of zombies. And many people are familiar with the zombies found in the very popular video game *Minecraft* (2011).

Hopefully, a zombie invasion will never occur in the real world. Video games, however, give people the opportunity to

At conventions, fans often do cosplay as favorite video game characters. Here are cosplays of a Creeper from Minecraft (*left*) and a Licker from Resident Evil (*right*). Both characters are zombies.

test their survival instincts without having to worry about being inducted into the horde and turning on their own friends and loved ones!

WALKING AND RUNNING WITH THE DEAD

Zombies may not exist outside of our imaginations, but for many people, the next best thing is getting involved in a pretend zombie event. As zombie runs gain popularity, event organizers and groups around the world are creating more and more end-of-the-world competitions and survival games that pit people against "zombies."

Zombie runs have been around for several years. It's not clear how these events started, but most likely, zombie runs began with individuals or local community organizations seeking to put a new—and fun—spin on the 5K run. A 5K run is a running competition where participants complete a distance of 5 kilometres (3.1 miles). 5Ks are often hosted for pure competitive reasons or to raise money for charities.

At a zombie survival run, participants often take the role of survivor or citizen and race against each other to outrun zombies. The zombies are generally played by event staff or participants who are selected or volunteer to play the role. The goal is to reach the finish line before becoming infected by a zombie. Once infected, which can involve having a colored flag stolen by a zombie, the participant is either out of the race or becomes a zombie herself and tries to infect other runners.

There are several variations to the rules and gameplay of a zombie run. Additionally, zombie runs are not limited to athletic competitions. Some zombie runs are events where everyone plays the role of a zombie. Other more complex events, can take place in large designated areas, such as abandoned warehouses, where participants have to survive for a certain amount of time or complete a certain number of tasks to win.

Following the increased popularity of zombies in pop culture in recent years, so many zombie runs are being planned world-wide that there is more than likely one happening in a city near you. Maybe even in your own community.

CHAPTER TWO

GETTING INVOLVED IN A ZOMBIE RUN

Zombie runs and similar events are being held in cities and local communities all around the world. It seems that no matter how different some cultures may be, zombies are a shared topic of interest. However, if you want to participate in a zombie run, there is a lot of preparation that must be done, including making a costume and even physically preparing for this kind of outdoor event. The kind of preparation you need depends on what kind of zombie run you will be participating in and where it will be. In the following sections, we will discuss how you can get involved, prepare, and hopefully survive your first zombie run.

FINDING THE ZOMBIE ACTION

It's rare that you will see a zombie run event advertised on television or hear about it on the radio. The most common place to find out about a zombie run or similar event is on the Internet. Many event organizers use social media, such as Facebook

Zombie run organizers and enthusiasts generally rely on word-of-mouth and social media to raise awareness of planned events.

and Twitter, to let people know about their event and to invite participants. Additionally, the organization that is hosting the zombie run may create a website dedicated to the event. As a participant, you first need to find these pages to learn about the event and how you can sign up.

Using a search website, such as Bing! or Google, you can easily find the websites and social media pages related to zombie runs in your area. To do this, simply type in "zombie run" and the name of your hometown or a nearby city to perform the search. This will bring up pages about events in or near that area, including past and future ones.

When you do find an event that is nearby, the first thing you should do is check for that group's requirements. There may be age or health restrictions on who can participate. Many zombie runs are for adults only, but you can search for family- and kid-friendly events. Always be sure to have your parent's or guardian's permission before signing up for anything online, especially when providing personal information such as a name or address during registration. Another requirement for participation may be a small fee, or getting sponsors, especially if this is a charity zombie run. It's important to follow the event rules to ensure that you can participate in any event you discover.

THE FINEST TATTERED RAGS

Possibly the most fun part about getting involved with a zombie run is getting to dress the part. In some non-competitive events, every participant dresses up as a zombie.

To prepare a costume, just remember that in zombie lore, these creatures could be any person at all. Zombies were once living people, and they all had different jobs and personalities. So, zombie costumes can be almost anything, including cops, construction workers, nurses, football players...you get the idea. Getting a costume together to play the role of a zombie is really not difficult at all.

You can probably find most of your costume in your own closet. Thrift stores are also good places to find interesting clothing, such as cheap suits and shirts that can be ripped up and covered in fake blood. In movies, the clothes worn by zombies are rarely in good condition. That may have to do with the

Putting together a scary zombie costume doesn't have to cost a lot of money. Old clothes and a little makeup can easily turn anyone into a perfect brain-eating zombie.

fact that they may have been partially eaten by another zombie or climbed up out of their own grave.

When you have the clothes that you want to use as your costume, you can then begin to zombiefy them. To do this, you can either rip them in strategic places, or use scissors to make jagged cuts in pants and shirts so that they look like they were clawed through. Additionally, zombie clothing usually has a bit of blood from where they were attacked. Red food coloring is a good and easy way to create blood-stained clothing. You can also use dark red liquids such as cranberry juice, even red markers if nothing else is available. Adding bloodied handprints is always eye-catching.

PERFECTING YOUR ZOMBIE LOOK

Once you've gotten your costume together, the next step in turning into a true zombie is to apply makeup and maybe even adding some special effects. If you've ever watched a zombie movie, you'll know that most of the time their skin is pallid from the loss of blood.

Some enthusiasts take their zombie costumes to the next level by using complex makeup techniques to create a realistic appearance.

Applying a lighter shade of foundation makeup than your regular skin tone to your face and exposed skin will give that un-healthy look that zombies are known for. To accent your cheeks and eyes, you can apply dark eye shadow to strategic places such as under the eyes and under the cheekbones to make your face look hollowed-out. This will give you a more lifeless appearance. If you don't have makeup at your disposal, you can add baby powder to your face and skin to make it appear ashen and dull.

For blood, you can use dark red lipstick. Simply apply it to your face in areas where you want to look bloodied. Remember that blood often drips, so make it look as though blood is flowing down your face. You can also apply bits of even darker lipsticks, such as maroon and purple, to make it look like the blood has dried up. Before your zombie run, you should practice different looks with your makeup to be sure to get the look you are hoping to achieve. Play around with different ideas and see which one you like best.

GETTING INTO CHARACTER

Depending on the type of zombie run you sign up to do, partic-ipants may be required to be a zombie or survivor. Part of the experience of being in a zombie run is becoming the character you play. When participants don't act out their role, they can take away from the experience of others.

Fortunately, playing the role of a zombie or survivor is not that challenging. Many zombie events don't involve running at all. Embracing the slow-movement of the zombies in *The*

Walking Dead, participants may actually drag along together through a route. These events often happen on streets that have been closed off to traffic. Participants limp along, make moaning noises, and snarl at onlookers.

In events where participants are being chased by zombies, they have to take on the role of a survivor. Survivors, of course, are fleeing from the zombies and are quite scared of being caught. To be a good survivor, it's best to keep moving.

When everyone is dressed for the event and has committed to playing their role, a zombie run can be very exciting for participants and onlookers.

THAT'S A LOT OF ZOMBIES

Zombie events that are well-planned can draw large numbers of participants. In 2012, around 25,000 people took part in the Argentina Zombie Walk that was held in the capital of Buenos Aires. Held annually, the purpose of the walk is to raise awareness for various social causes, including hunger. Participants in the yearly event are encouraged to bring food items that are then donated to shelters and those in need. Events such as the one in Argentina happen frequently to raise awareness to the problems faced by communities around the world. The benefit is that people get to have fun and help others at the same time.

ZOMBIE RUN TRAINING

Competitive zombie runs and other types of competitive zombie events require a certain level of athletic ability. Running in a 5K may sound like a simple run, but it is not as easy as it may sound if you are a beginner. In more difficult events like a triathlon, participants compete in three different stages, usually running, swimming, and bike riding.

Before signing up for a zombie run that involves a lot of physical activity, be sure to ask for permission from a parent or guardian. Next, you should begin training in order to build

Zombie walks, unlike zombie runs, are better suited for individuals that have not had much training in physical fitness and long-distance running events. This picture is from the Argentina Zombie Walk in 2012.

up your endurance and strength. For an event that requires only running, you will need to train by going on daily jogs or runs around your neighborhood. Start with a short distance and gradually increase to the distance of the event. Just remember that it is always safer to run in a group than on your own. Try to get a family member to go with you, or use a community track where a lot of people run and walk. Once you can do the distance, time your runs daily to see how your time improves.

At your home, you can do many different exercises to strengthen your body. Sit-ups and crunches are great ways to toughen up your abdominal, or stomach, area. If you have a pull-up bar, you can work on your arm strength.

For people who have access to a pool, swimming laps is an excellent way to build up endurance. This will help you maintain your strength throughout a run so that you don't become tired early on. Remember, only the fittest survive a zombie attack!

SURVIVING A ZOMBIE RUN

Being athletic will come in very handy, but there are also other ways that participants can make it to the finish line "alive."

One of the best methods of surviving a zombie run is to work in groups. Zombies will have to go after one person at a time. As a team, you can decide who will distract the zombies so that other team members can continue on. If you do enter a zombie run alone, you can try to make friends before the event begins. If you're lucky enough, the zombies will eat your team-mates first!

CHAPTER THREE

START YOUR OWN ZOMBIE RUN

While it's fun to be part of a zombie run, you may also decide you want to run your own. Starting your own zombie run or fitness event can be fun and profitable. However, there are many things you have to do in order to make your event a success. Because people may pay money to participate in an event, they will expect it to be well planned out. With the help of friends and family, you can run a well-organized event. You can even help charitable organizations plan their own zombie runs and walks rather than doing your own. In the following sections, we will discuss the basics of getting your zombie run together.

ORGANIZING YOUR FIRST RUN

Putting on a zombie run takes a lot of dedication and work. Large zombie runs can require months of preparation. Additionally, they can require several staff members to help run the event.

However, it can be relatively easy to put together a small-scale run with friends. The best part is that you can have fun and even make money at the same time, either for a charity or for yourself. Due to age requirements, it may be difficult to get a permit to host an event that takes place on public property, such as a park or city streets. Still, students can enlist the help of responsible adults to help take care of such challenges.

If you have access to an open area of land, such as a field or large lawn, you have a perfect place to host a zombie run. Some schools may even work with their students to host a 5K or short-distance run on school property. Using the help of friends,

Working together with friends to organize a zombie run or similar event can be both fun and rewarding.

there are many tasks that will need to be completed in order to have a successful run, including firming up a location for the event, deciding on a name, letting people know about the event (advertising), selling tickets, and getting sponsors, as well as dealing with the logistics of the day such as how people will get there, where they will check in, what is the route or rules for the run, and what the winners or what all participants will receive at the end. Remember, it's also important to have first aid on hand as well as water, food, and bathroom facilities.

This may seem like a lot to have to think about, so if organizing a zombie run is too challenging, you may also find opportunities to work at an event. Working with people who have done it before is a good way to learn about all the different things involved in running such an event. Depending on your age, you may be able to offer help with different tasks, including handing out water to runners, playing a zombie, taking pictures, and registering participants.

TEAM UP FOR A GOOD CAUSE

Competitive events, such as 5Ks and triathlons, are great ways to raise money for good causes. In recent years, many charitable organizations have hosted 5K competitions and walks to raise awareness.

One of the most popular 5K and fitness events is the Susan G. Komen Race for the Cure. Held annually in communities around the world, the events raise awareness and funds to aid research and treatment of breast cancer.

ZOMBIE FLASH MOB

Could there be anything more shocking than to see a large group of zombies suddenly show up out of nowhere? A flash mob is a gathering of people in a public area who perform a random act, such as dancing or singing together. Recently, zombies have also been making their way into flash mob popularity.

In 2013, a mob of forty men and women dressed up as zombies gathered in the town square of Portland, Maine. To the shock of bystanders, the zombies weren't hungry for brains. Instead, they were hungry for dance. In unison, the zombies performed pop artist Michael Jackson's famous dance routine to the song "Thriller." As soon as the song and dance were over, the zombies crawled and staggered home.

Most cities and towns are home to a variety of charity groups dedicated to causes such as hunger and veteran care. Your own community probably has several organizations that you may not even know about.

Increasingly, more of these organizations are hosting runs and fitness events. While this is great, it also means that many participants are limited to the number of events they can financially support. For that reason, organizations are looking for more ways to make their events different from the rest.

Given the current popularity of zombies in pop culture, hosting zombie runs and walks are great ways to stand out from the usual fundraising events. Groups often need help in assisting with running events and promoting them. Many

Zombie runs and events don't always have to raise money. Charitable organizations can often benefit from the publicity they receive from just organizing or participating in an event.

people have not even heard of zombie runs, which means you can bring new ideas to a group that will be embraced.

Since charitable organizations rely on donations and volunteers, it is often easy to get involved. To join up with a charitable organization, parents and teachers are often the best place to ask for contacts to group leaders and organizers. Searching the Internet for organization websites and social media pages is also a quick way to find contact information.

Setting the Rules

There are many different ways to put together a zombie run or fitness event. First, organizers should ask themselves who their target audience is. Events that involve a lot of physical activity such as running and going through obstacles may not be a good fit for most people. Triathlons and 5Ks, for example, may not be a good fit for children. Walking events, however, can appeal to just about anyone.

For a zombie walk, the rules are pretty simple. Mainly, the participants have to dress up as zombies. Second, a walking event is not a competition. Therefore, participants can take their time getting from the starting line to the finish line.

Competitive runs and events, however, will require more thought when it comes to rules. If the goal of your event is to get to the finish line alive, you will need to set guidelines.

For example, one of the easiest ways to separate survivors from zombies is to use flags. Rather than eating a participant, the zombie has to grab a flag or piece of fabric that is on the survivor. The flag can be attached using Velcro or by putting it on a belt. Once the survivor has lost his or her flag, that person becomes a zombie and has to get other people's flags.

For safety reasons, it is very important to make rules for how people act during the event. For example, pushing and shoving should never be allowed. Because competitive events can be dangerous, it's important to have an adult around who knows first aid in case someone gets hurt.

PLANNING OUT THE COURSE

Well before the day of the event, organizers need to decide on the course for a zombie run or event. Depending on the type of event, the course will vary. However, in all cases, the organizers should walk through the entire course to check for any obstacles or problems that could injure or cause difficulty for a large group of participants, such as uneven ground, narrow spaces, debris, or other issues from neighboring structures.

A 5K, for example, will require enough space for groups of people to be able to run together and pass each other. If you

A zombie run course has to be thought out and tested well-ahead of the actual event. It's important to make sure the course is safe and large enough to accommodate all participants.

live in a small town, you may be lucky enough to be able to use a local park or streets that are roped off for the event. To measure the distance of a course, you can use a pedometer. A pedometer is a device that measures distance while walking or running. They can be bought at sports and fitness stores or even purchased as an app on a smartphone. If your course is a jogging trail at a local park, you will need to figure out how many times around the trail will equal 3.1 miles (5 kilometers).

If you organize or help with an event that uses obstacles, you may need to design the obstacles. You can make obstacles that participants have to climb over by placing stacks of hay bales throughout the course. Mud pits are also fun obstacles to create that will slow down survivors.

Additionally, you can even create parts of the course that require participants to complete a puzzle or task. For instance, before moving on from a certain point, the survivor might have to answer three trivia questions about zombie movies correctly.

There are many ways to make a zombie event fun for participants. The only limit is the organizer's imagination.

PROMOTING YOUR ZOMBIE RUN

Setting up the course and making rules might be the most challenging part to organizing a zombie run. Nonetheless, one of the most important tasks is to promote your event.

Luckily, the Internet makes it possible to reach large numbers of people without having to spend a lot of money. Using social networks, such as Facebook, Instagram, Twitter, or Tumblr, you can create an event page to raise awareness. Your event page should include information on what the event is for, the rules, location, date, and registration information. Additionally, if there are restrictions, such as age limits, you should make that known. To promote the page, you can ask friends and family to share links to it on their profiles.

Keep in mind, however, that not everyone uses social media. To market your event further, you can print fliers and put them around your community. Many public places, such as libraries and town halls, have boards where local residents can post notices of events. Local radio stations and newspapers may also be willing to make announcements about your event free of charge.

Of course, one of the easiest ways to get your event known in the community is simply by word of mouth. Tell your friends, family, and anyone you know to spread the word.

CHAPTER FOUR

THE LIFE OF A PROFESSIONAL ZOMBIE

As you've probably already noted in the previous sections, zombie runs can be very involved. The people participating and organizing them have to use a lot of different skills to ensure a successful event. Getting involved with zombie runs can be used to open doors to many different careers. In the following sections, we'll discuss different jobs that can benefit from experience with zombie runs.

ACTORS AND EXTRAS

If you've ever watched the television series *The Walking Dead,* you probably know that it takes a lot of actors to make up the hordes of zombies. In the film and television industry, these people are known as extras. They usually don't talk on camera. Instead, they are used in the background of scenes in a variety of movies and television shows. Their job may involve pretending to eat dinner at a restaurant, silently "talking" in the background, or walking down a city sidewalk.

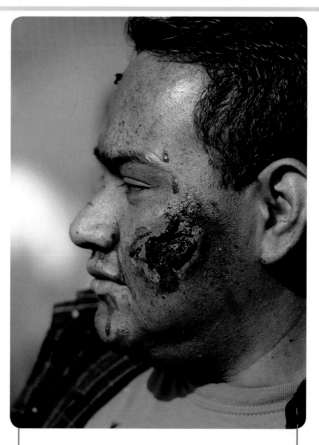

Many actors, such as the stars of *The Walking Dead*, got their start in the film industry by being extras. Getting into an acting career can be difficult. It requires determination and courage to truly succeed. Getting involved in school plays and in local community theaters is a good start to making your way to Hollywood.

If you really have a desire to become an actor or actress, you can get the help of an acting coach. An acting coach's job is to prepare aspiring actors for auditions and to improve their talents on stage. However, adding a stint as a zombie in a zombie run on your headshot can also be beneficial as it shows

This participant in a zombie run could translate the experience into an acting job using pictures of his zombie role.

working acting credit, even if you weren't paid for the event.

MAKEUP, COSTUME, AND SET DESIGNERS

Even with the best actors, a movie is not complete if it doesn't look real. To complete the movie, makeup artists and set and costume designers transform the ordinary into the extraordinary.

Makeup artists often use more than just lipstick and foundation to turn people into zombies and monsters. They have to know how to create all sorts of facial features and fake body parts in order to scare an audience. This includes creating masks with a rubbery product called latex and even making wigs by hand. Makeup artists are masters of detail and understand that every a fake bruise or bloodstain has to be unique.

Another career path that may involve working with zombie films is costume designing. Costume designers are responsible for picking out and even creating by hand the clothes that an actor or actress wears. In one movie, they may create tattered

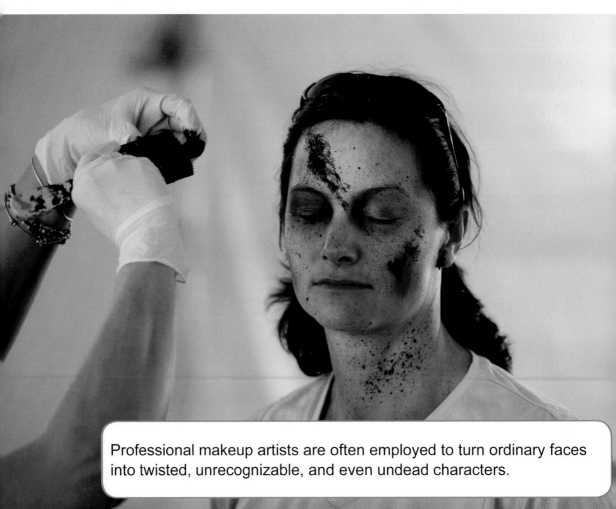

Professional makeup artists are often employed to turn ordinary faces into twisted, unrecognizable, and even undead characters.

clothes for a zombie. In another, they may tailor fancy dresses for a film that takes place in a king's court.

A third career option in film is that of set designer. Set designers scout for places where a scene can be filmed if it is being filmed outdoors, and then they create the sets to fit into that outdoor location. If the filming is being done indoors, they create the set, including all the background themselves. They have to use good artistic judgment to make sure that the set fits the time and location of the movie. Sets might have to be life-sized, including abandoned towns or even space stations. People who have worked on designing or decorating a zombie run course might be able to translate the skills they learned into working as a set designer.

EVENT ORGANIZERS

Following a path in event organization can lead to many different career opportunities. From weddings to haunted houses to festivals, there is no shortage of choices. As a young person, there are plenty of ways to get started.

Zombie runs and other fitness events, for instance, require a lot of planning. Event organizers have to hire staff and sometimes train them to do their jobs. They also have to make sure that there are enough costumes for everyone. Additionally, they ensure that courses or designated areas for the event are reserved. Young people can provide assistance to organizers to gain experience.

Outside of planning zombie runs, event planning is a career path of its own. Event planners are responsible for putting together large events, such as music festivals or science fiction

ZOMBIE GENRE WRITERS

Behind every zombie movie and book there is a writer. From their minds, the dead walk again and infect the living. A career in writing can be challenging when it comes to making money. However, it can also be very personally rewarding. Consider that all of the movies and television shows you have watched involved a writer. Robert Kirkman, the creator of the comic book series *The Walking Dead*, was originally interested in drawing. However, he soon realized at a young age that he was better at writing. Today, *The Walking Dead* television series is one of the most popular television shows.

conventions. This requires everything from choosing and renting out a location, handling logistics such as lighting, speakers, and air conditioning, building sets or setting up booth spaces, advertising the event so that it brings in organizations to display their products and services to fans and customers, and coordinating schedules of guest speakers and making sure that staff members are doing their jobs.

JOBS IN MARKETING

Without marketing, people would not know about products and events that are being sold. It is the responsibility of marketing professionals to get the word out. They have a variety of jobs, which may include writing, graphic design, working on television commercials, and managing social media accounts.

Getting hired into a marketing company usually requires a degree in marketing or similar job experience. Volunteering with local charitable organizations is a great way to start building your own experience. For one, you can provide help with a social media account. Many organizations fail to take full advantage of social media. Your experience getting the word out about a local zombie run might be just what they need to reach new customers.

Creating print advertisements requires creativity as well as graphic design skills. Graphic designers use design software to create memorable ads that can be used on the Internet and

Your creativity as a writer, designer, or social media manager could translate into working at a marketing agency or in the marketing department of a company to help promote their events and products.

in newspapers and magazines. Designers who work with video may also help in creating commercials for the Internet or for television.

Marketing is an important aspect of most businesses that sell products or services directly to customers. As long as there is something to sell or raise awareness of, there will be jobs in marketing.

ADDITIONAL EVENT ROLES

Zombie runs and physical fitness events can range in size. Some events may have very few participants. Others may have thousands of participants.

Events such as the New York City Marathon utilize a variety of staff for different jobs. Security is very important at events that have lots of participants. A job in security may require training in how to deal with a belligerent person and how to respond to emergency situations. Medics are also a vital part of competitive events. Accidents on the course may require the help of an individual that has training in life-saving skills, such as CPR.

Because crowds often gather for big competitive events, there are other job duties that can be fulfilled. For example, cooks may be hired to work concession stands. Announcers who can narrate the event may be hired to provide coverage for radio.

Finding a career that specializes only in zombies may be difficult. Nonetheless, an interest in the walking dead can lead to different opportunities that you may never have thought of.

assassination The murder of someone of importance by surprise or secret attack.

charity An organization that helps and raises money for those in need.

endurance The length of time and ability to withstand physical activity such as exercise.

foundation A cream or powder that gives facial skin an even appearance before applying other cosmetics.

genre A particular type of music, art, or literature.

horde A group of wandering people.

lore Knowledge or traditions on a subject that are held by a group of people.

mainstream Ideas, interests, or attitudes that are popular among society for different periods of time.

marketing Promoting or selling a product or service through different means, such as advertising.

origin The point or place where something begins.

plague A mass outbreak of a disease among people that is highly deadly.

plantation A property where crops such as corn and coffee are grown by resident laborers.

reanimated To have been brought back to life after death.

slave A person who is owned by another person against his or her will.

sorcerer An individual who claims or is believed to have magical powers.

trance A state of mind where the individual is unaware of his or her surroundings.

Costume Designers Guild
11969 Ventura Boulevard, 1st Floor
Studio City, CA 91604
(818) 752-2400
Website: http://www.costumedesignersguild.com
The Costume Designers Guild is an organization of more than 800 professionals that promotes research, artistry, and technical expertise in costume design in the field of motion pictures.

The Event Planners Association (EPA)
25432 Trabuco, Suite 207
Lake Forest, CA 92630
(866) 380-3372
Website: http://www.eventplannersassociation.com
The EPA is an American trade organization dedicated to providing support to independent event organizers and businesses through legal and marketing support. The organization also hosts industry events for professionals to network.

National Association for Health and Fitness (NAHF)
10 Kings Mill Court
Albany, NY 12205-3632
(518) 456-1058
Website: http://www.physicalfitness.org
The mission of the NAHF is to improve the quality of life for individuals by promoting physical fitness and encouraging active lifestyles.

Screen Actors Guild (SAG)
5757 Wilshire Boulevard, 7th Floor
Los Angeles, CA 90036-3600
(323) 954-1600
Website: http://www.sagaftra.org
The SAG represents more than 160,000 professionals within
the acting and film industries to protect individuals from
unfair treatment in the work environment.

The YMCA
101 North Wacker Drive
Chicago, IL 60606
(800) 872-9622
Website: http://www.ymca.net
The YMCA is a nationwide nonprofit organization that promotes healthy lifestyles and encourages physical activity
among American youth.

WEBSITES

Because of the changing nature of Internet links, Rosen Publishing has developed an online list of websites related
to the subject of this book. This site is updated regularly.
Please use this link to access the list:

http://www.rosenlinks.com/RPFP/Zombie

Bailey, Diane. Zombies in America (America's Supernatural Secrets). New York, NY: Rosen Central, 2011.

Blattner, Don. Health, Wellness, and Physical Fitness, Grades 5-8. Greensboro, NC: Carson-Dellosa Publishing Group, 2013.

Colson, Mary. Being a Makeup Artist (On the Radar: Awesome Jobs). Minneapolis, MN: Lerner Publications, 2012.

Craig, Jonathan, and Bridget Light. Special Effects Make-up Artist: The Coolest Jobs on the Planet. Basingstoke, Hampshire, UK: Raintree Publishing, 2013.

Dabrowski, Kristen. My First Monologue Book: 100 Monologues for Young Children (Young Actors). Portland, ME: Smith & Kraus, 2007.

Dakota, Heather. Zombie Apocalypse Survival Guide. New York, NY: Scholastic Paperback Nonfiction, 2011.

Frederick, Shane. Speed Training for Teen Athletes. North Mankato, MN: Capstone Press, 2014.

Guillain, Charlotte. 101 Ways to Get in Shape. Basingstoke, Hampshire, UK: Raintree Publishing, 2011.

Hamilton, S. L. Zombies (Xtreme Monsters). Edina, MN: ABDO Publishing, 2010.

Mason, Helen. Makeup Artist (Creative Careers). New York, NY: Gareth Stevens Publishing, 2014.

Mayfield, Katherine. Acting A to Z: The Young Person's Guide to a Stage or Screen Career. New York, NY: Random House, 2010.

Owen, Ruth. Zombies and Other Walking Dead (Not Near Normal: The Paranormal). New York, NY: Bearport Publishing, 2013.

Regan, Lisa. Vampires, Werewolves & Zombies. New York, NY: Scholastic Books, 2009.

Shone, Rob. Zombies: Tales of the Living Dead (Graphic Tales of the Supernatural). New York, NY: Rosen Central, 2011.

Shryer, Donna, and Jodi Forschmiedt. Peak Performance: Sports Nutrition (Benchmark Rockets). New Rochelle, NY: Benchmark Education, 2009.

Akner-Brodesser, Taffy. "Max Brooks Is Not Kidding About the Zombie Apocalypse." New York Times Magazine. June 21, 2013. Retrieved May 4, 2015 (http://www.nytimes.com/2013/06/23/magazine/max-brooks-is-not-kidding-about-the-zombie-apocalypse.html).

Encyclopaedia Britannica. "George A. Romero." February 27, 2014. Retrieved May 3, 2015 (http://www.britannica.com/EBchecked/topic/1695444/George-A-Romero).

Hoey, Dennis. "Zombie Flash Mob Invades Portland for 'Thriller' Dance." Portland Press Herald, October 24, 2013. Retrieved May 3, 2015 (http://www.pressherald.com/2013/10/24/it_s_a_zombie_thrill/).

Lakshmi, Ghandi. "Zoinks! Tracing the History of 'Zombie' from Haiti to the CDC." National Public Radio, December 15, 2013. Retrieved May 1, 2015 (http://www.npr.org/sections/codeswitch/2013/12/13/250844800/zoinks-tracing-the-history-of-zombie-from-haiti-to-the-cdc).

Peisner, David. "Robert Kirkman: I Can Do 1,000 Issues of 'The Walking Dead.'" Rolling Stone, October 8, 2013. Retrieved May 5, 2015 (http://www.rollingstone.com/tv/news/robert-kirkman-i-can-do-1-000-issues-of-the-walking-dead-20131008).

Radford, Benjamin. "Zombies: The Real Story of the Undead." Live Science, October 10, 2012. Retrieved May 2, 2015 (http://www.livescience.com/23892-zombies-real-facts.html).

Thompson, Matt. "Why Black Heroes Make Zombie Stories More Interesting." National Public Radio, October 1, 2013. Retrieved May 1, 2015 (http://www.npr.org/sections/codeswitch/2013/09/30/227943197/why-black-heroes-make-zombie-stories-more-interesting).

About the Author

Joe Greek is a nonfiction writer from Tennessee. He has written books for young adults on several topics, including social media and 3D printing. He is an avid fan of zombie films, especially the works of George A. Romero. In his spare time, he enjoys exercising and running in order to physically prepare for a possible zombie invasion.

Photo Credits

Cover Andreas Gradin/Shutterstock.com; pp. 4-5 Josep Lago/AFP/Getty Images; p. 8 Jerry Cooke/The LIFE Images Collection/Getty Images; p. 13 Dan Kitwood/Getty Images; p. 17 Lucas Oleniuk/Toronto Star/Getty Images; p. 19 Ethan Miller/Getty Images; p. 20 J. Vespa/WireImage/Getty Images; p. 23 Grupo13/CON/LatinContent Editorial/Getty Images; p. 26 RyFlip/Shutterstock.com; p. 29 Tomasz Bidermann/Shutterstock.com; pp. 31, 35, 36 Andy Cross/The Denver Post/Getty Images; p. 39 michaeljung/Shutterstock.com
Designer: Brian Garvey; Editor/Photo Researcher: Tracey Baptiste